LAUGHTER & *TEARS*

BRIAN AUSTIN

Laughter & Tears
Copyright 2005

www.UndiscoveredTreasures.org
282906 R.R. #3
Durham, Ont., CAN
N0G 1R0

Poetry and text by Brian Austin
Photographs as indicated in End Notes on page 95

© 2005 ISBN: 1-894928-66-0

Printed by Word Alive Press
for
Undiscovered Treasures
All rights reserved

Special thanks to Carolyn Wilker
Editor & fellow poet.
Apologies for the stubbornness that has resisted some of her suggestions.

Cover design by Nikki Braun

Table of Contents

DEDICATION v

CELEBRATING FAMILY
  What Is a Belly-Button For?.. 2
  A Tornado Lives At Our House 4
  A Mother's Love 6
  A Little Thing 9
  Not for the Timid 10

FOR THE ROMANTICALLY IMPAIRED
  A Hot, Hot Date 12
  Susie's Beau 14

THE JOYS AND TRIAL OF LIFE
  The Waiting Room 17
  The Unraveling 18
  A Coat of Faded Colours 20
  Youth Ministry 23
  Blaming God 24
  The Undaunted 28
  Checking Out Hell 32
  Day of Darkness 34
  Where God Works 37
  In the Storm 38
  Homeless Trilogy   A Bed of Roses 40
                                  Homeless? 42
                                  The Ventilation Grate 44
  No Room For Tears 46
  A Cup of Cool Water 47

FOR GRIEVING HEARTS
  Forever 49
  Dylan 50
  The Weariness of Sorrow 52

Farewell Little One 54
In the Darkest Hour 55
Grief 56
Shared Tears 58
The Echo of My Weeping 61
I Faced a Man 62
Unwanted 63
Even for the Damned 64

CELEBRATING THE COMING
Grumpy Santa 68
Love Revealed 70
No Vacancy 72

ON A LIGHTER NOTE
Eye Teeth 76
Meddling Trilogy   The Weed 78
                                    The Hunk 80
                                    Hell's Laughter 82
The Last Goodbye 84
Nitroglycerine 86
What's Growing in Your Clutter? 87

ALPHABETICAL INDEX 88

FIRST LINE INDEX 89

ENDNOTES 90

ABOUT THE AUTHOR 91

AUTHOR'S NOTE 92

*Dedicated
to the memory
of
Dylan Michael Edgcumbe
whose coming we celebrated
for only five days*

Photo by Jason Edgcumbe [1]

Celebrating Family

Photo by Alanna Rusnak [2]

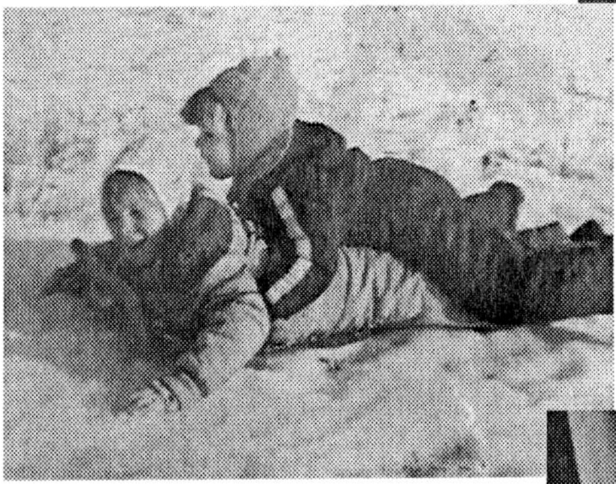

Photo by Brian Austin [3]

Photo by Alanna Rusnak [2]

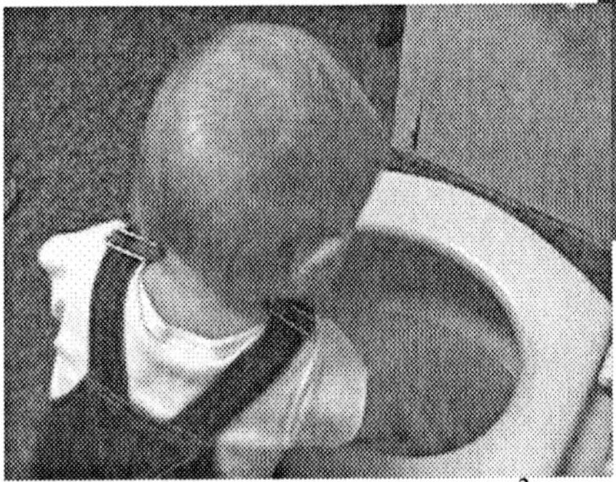

Photo by Alanna Rusnak [2]

Laughter & Tears

What Is a Belly-Button For?

I've got a belly-button.
I don't know what it's for.
It looks a little bit like
the lock on our front door.

I tried a lot of keys out.
None of them seemed to fit,
but I giggled and I wiggled
cause they tickled quite a bit.

I'm made so very special.
Mom says it's God's design.
I don't know what some parts are for
but I like them still just fine.

I have two little pinky toes.
There's one on both my feet.
They help me count higher than ten
and they do look kind of neat.

When Grandma tries to tickle them,
I laugh and run away,
or I wiggle and I giggle
as close to her I stay.

I've got so many pieces.
I don't know what they do.
I think God made a puzzle.
Did He make you that way too?

Brian Austin

My tongue can make strange faces
or taste an ice-cream cone.
My ears are made just perfect
for when Grandma's on the phone.

But what good's a belly-button?
That's what I want to see,
and I giggle and I wiggle
as I try another key.

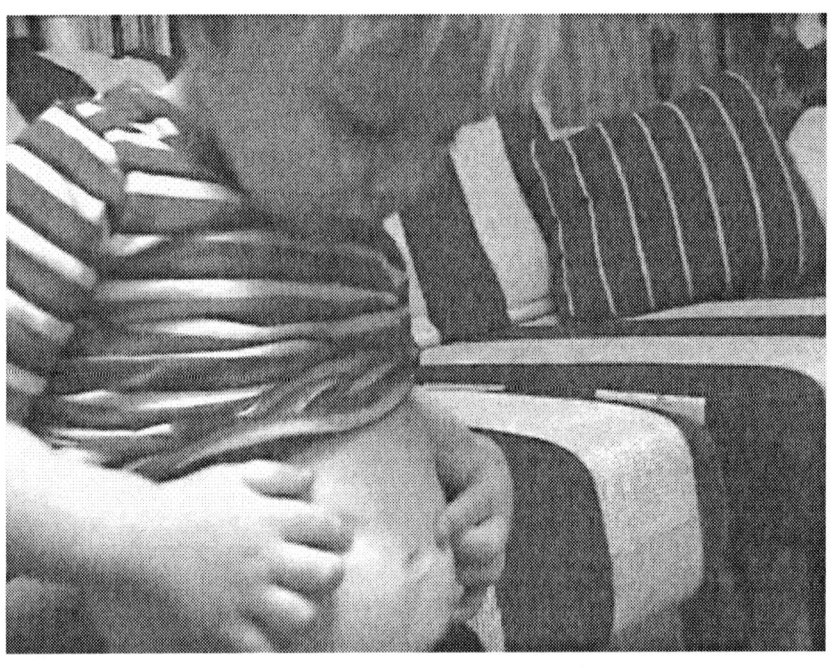

Photo by Alanna Rusnak [2]

A Tornado Lives at Our House

There lives a small tornado
by the highway on the hill
and blows through our house
ten dozen times a day.
It will sit right through a story
if you turn the pages fast,
but if too slow,
it'll spin itself away.

You can pick up toys and papers,
and books and this and that's;
have the whole house looking
neat as a pin,
when like a spinning dervish,
the tornado will blow through
and howl with glee
o'er a contest you can't win.

You can scrub around the high-chair,
where things are sticking to the floor.
You can wash the peas and gravy
off the wall.
You can sit down for a cup of tea
on a quiet afternoon,
but the tornado
will in that moment call.

*You can sterilize the bottle,
but it'll suck things off the floor.
You can sweep and mop and vacuum
day and night.
But the tornado will get the best of you.
You might as well give in
and just love the little whirlwind
spinning bright.*

*Ah, love – yes that's the secret,
though something's sticking to your shoes
and chocolate pudding kisses
leave their mark.
And you've read the story a dozen times,
but the whirlwind asks again,
on its endless race
from sunrise until dark.*

*A tornado lives at our house,
and blows through so very oft'
and we don't know how we lived
before it came.
We give hugs when we can catch it;
read stories o'er and o'er,
and delight to hear
the little whirlwind's name.*

Photo by Brian Austin. [3]

A Mother's Love

*Love so oft' is stripped of all.
the strength behind the name.
Just a warm and fuzzy feeling,
or a playboy's midnight fling.*

*But a mother bear who cuffs her cub
and sends him up a tree,
then turns with snarling, yellowed fangs
to face an enemy,*

*or a hen with maligned, pea-sized brain
who crouches on a nest
while dog with blood-lust blindly kills,
covers babies 'neath her breast,*

*both act with love that's rarely found
'mong "nobler" human kind.
They act when cooler minds would quail
'gainst the perils they might find.*

*A mother returning to a fire
to rescue her small child
shows love as great as anything
among creatures small or wild.*

*But what of those who day by day
endure the daily grind
of humble tasks and labours dull
that stir no poet's mind?*

*Through endless loads of dirty clothes,
through meals and wrinkled beds,
a sigh escapes a mother's lips
as she kisses sleeping heads.*

*She's laboured through the hours again.
Thank-yous have been few.
She'd love the chance to lie and soak
or read a book right through.*

*Her husband's cool and distant now
though not from planned intent.
He's preoccupied with scattered toys
and the cash they represent.*

*From nine to five he's done his stint.
Now there's Johnny's bike to fix.
The TV and the paper call.
He'd like supper at six.*

*A mother's love has a high price tag.
Few men could pay the bill.
Hard as they try, they just can't see
needs moms routinely fill.*

*To husband, father, myself too,
I'd whisper a word:
"Hold high the value of your wife.
Give thanks in act and word."*

*You'll never know what her love's worth
unless someday it's gone.
Those mundane tasks she does for you
through weary hours and long . . .*

*may not feel like love to you,
may in fact seem rather dull,
but if you count their real worth
you'll know that she stands tall.*

*A mother's love is a treasure sure
found in hovel or mansion bright.
In all our homes there's a thanks deserved,
tired eyes to fill with light.*

*You cannot pay the price it'd cost
to purchase a mother's love,
but you can say "Thanks," and share a task
and value what she does.*

*Love so oft is stripped of all
the strength behind the name.
But a mother's love is a strength indeed
of humble, unsung fame.*

*Whether mundane task or in anger bold
as fierce as a mother bear,
you'll search this world far and wide
for a strength that dares compare*

*with the unsung strength of a mother's love
through the seasons of her life.
I know it's true! I'm one who's blessed.
One of those mothers is my wife.*

Brian Austin

A Little Thing

It seemed to be so little
to those who just looked on.
We had no hint of a prayerful plea
of a mother for her son.

No hint we would be witness
to that which seems so rare,
a very simple answer
to a very focused prayer.

The giver had no inkling
of the blessing from her hands.
She gave what she was able
unfolding God's own plans.

We caught a glimpse of glory.
We felt His warm embrace
when we saw a mother's wonder
and the tears that wet her face.

For what seemed to us so little
to her was answered prayer.
Just an old and time-worn fiddle,
yet it proved God's loving care.

Not For the Timid

Not for the timid yet what delight
as you stretch your wings in fledgling flight.

How rich the privilege! What honour rare!
To be close by as you take to the air.

How did God dare to give to us
such an awesome task? Such a timeless trust?

For who can show any greater task
than to raise a child, set you free at last

To soar to heights only God can know
as with tear-filled eyes we bid you go.

The applause of Heaven is yours to seek
as prayer vigil your parents keep.

Not for the timid, yet, tis honour true.
We thank God for trusting us with you.

Brian Austin

For the

Romantically

Impaired

A Hot, Hot Date

T'was a hot, hot date.
She was young and sweet.
Her dad was a nervous wreck.
And he thought he'd take a certain guy
by the scrawny, scruffy neck
and hang him gently for an hour.
Perhaps he'd make it two,
just to give a hint, in a subtle way
of things that he might do
if his daughter came to grief that night
or came home in scalding tears,
if she told a tale in the aftermath
that burned her father's ears.

Now he liked the kid
that was plain to see
and he'd use a padded rope.
He'd slacken the noose now and then
to give a breath to the poor bloke.
And he really didn't want to have him
scared to hang around.
But he thought it well – you should agree
to set the rules right from the ground.

T'was a hot, hot date.
She was young and sweet.
Her boyfriend was six foot four.
Dad raised his gaze to meet the eyes
of that youth outside the door.

And he shook his hand with a nervous grin
joked a father's gray-haired way.
And he waved goodbye with a shaky sigh
as the old car pulled away.

And the rope is sitting in the truck.
And it never has been used.
And his mind goes back to those years ago
when another father mused
on the scruffy guy at his daughter's side
and the things he'd like to say
before that guy with a beat-up car
and his daughter drove away.

T'was a hot, hot date.
She was young and sweet.
Strange, how the years can fly!
He stole a hug from his old sweetheart
who still put up with this scruffy guy.

On-Line Dating Service.
Please Adjust your Web-Cam.
You're looking for a WHAT?

Laughter & Tears

Susie's Beau

I'm heading back to school again
an' I just don't wanna go.
They'll make me study algebra
an' stuff I don't need to know.

There's fishing off the river bank.
There's baseball in the park.
But I'll be doing homework
from supper until dark.

T'was the first day of school today
an' I didn't wanna go.
But Susie's got the desk beside
an' she's got a special glow.

There's swimming at the waterhole.
There's swinging from a tree.
But I'm dreaming dreams of Susie.
She looks like **Wow!!** to me.

Brian Austin

Yes I'm dreaming dreams of Susie.
Is she dreaming about me?
How can the clock be so darn slow?
Gotta get to school to see.

The guys'll be kicking footballs
or talking about girls.
But I'll be getting close to her.
Love the way that her hair curls.

Susie's seeing Tommy Jones.
He's the captain of the team.
He thinks he's really some cool dude
an' I just wanna scream.

They're bouncing with a basketball.
There's a water-fight in the park.
But I'm staring at a stack of books,
blinds pulled and bedroom dark.

I'm heading back to school again.
Why? I'd like to know.
What earthly good is pi-r-squared
if Susie has a beau?

The Joys and Trials of Life

Brian Austin

The Waiting Room

It's not a very pleasant room.
It's small and drab and dull.
The magazines are ten years old.
There are scuff marks on the wall.

No music masks the whirring hum
of fans, or voices stark
that rise and fall in muffled tones
like shadows in the dark.

Lacking substance, faceless, cold,
it's a room without a soul.
Asks mocking questions, flirts with dread,
"for whom does this bell toll?"

Terror grows in waiting rooms.
It feeds on nameless fears.
Strong man or child of tender years
oft' battle threatening tears.

But a giggle breaks the cursed calm
of pretense over fear.
A sigh escapes as dread fears fly.
A child's teasing voice we hear.

For life holds promise. Sweet the pain
of piercing little voice.
The waiting room's no longer dull.
A smile's our only choice.

The Unraveling

Piling up the sleepless nights. So too the endless days.
Mocks the order to "SHUT UP" – my mind torments.
Endless the recycling of disappointments and of wounds.
Endless the borrowing of tomorrow's pain –

– as if today had not enough,
and I call myself a fool.
My mind with bitter laughter gives assent.

I fight the tears that crowd too close, though I ache to let them flow,
while through endless pain-filled hours I cry within.

A life's work of love unravels – but I cannot catch the threads.
I'm a man! I'm strong! I will not stoop to tears.
But sobs my heart – in a language that no one seems to know.
I'm broken. Seems I'm bleeding. I'm so scared.

And I would cry with poetry – and break your heart as well
but rhyme and meter refuse to serve my ends.
So I would cry with stirring prose – but find broken, shattered words,
and the will to struggle on is almost gone.

The sun will rise tomorrow. That's what I tell myself,
but the knowledge just mocks the hurt within,
while a life's work of love unravels and I cannot catch the threads
and I ache to lay this heavy burden down.

But I have a task that's yet undone. The cup's not fully drained,
though I've tasted of its bitterness so deep.
My hands grasp – and fail. The threads slip fast away.
Bitter my despair. Sharp my grief.

But greater hands are weaving from what I counted loss.
No pattern yet, nor beauty can I see.
But the hands – scarred hands – I recognize, as pausing, they touch me –
bring comfort – though of answers offer none.

Still a life's work of love unravels and I cannot see the end.
But scarred hands are at work among the threads.
Almost I dare to hope again. Almost I dare to trust.
and from my frantic efforts – take my rest.

Photo by Brian Austin [3]

A Coat of Faded Colours
(Joseph's Diary)

Why, God?
Were the dreams just a stupid kid's imagination?
What am I doing in this hole?
Why was I so stupid to run away?
It wasn't as if she was so awful looking.
Is this my reward for trying to follow You?
She's the tramp, but I get blamed!
What kind of justice is that?

I suppose my brothers are all grandfathers by now,
and I'm locked up because I wouldn't share her bed.

Are You real, God?
Do You care?

Potiphar knows the truth.
He knows!
He'd have had me executed if he believed her.
Any husband would.

O God! I wanted so bad to give in!
I wanted so bad!
And this is my reward?
Why?
Two years I've slaved for him.
Two years!
Oh, I strutted.
I was proud,
like when I had those dreams;
proud because he'd put me over everything
except her.

Brian Austin

But I was still a slave!

God, I hate being a slave!
I hate being locked up!
I hate being guilty for something I didn't even do!
I hate the thinking that won't stop –
about what it would have felt like . . .
O God, Why?

How long, God?
What did the dreams mean anyway?
So I was a cocky young fool;
proud of my coat;
proud of being Dad's favorite;
proud of my dreams,
and sure I was headed for big things . . .
Big things? – Ha!!
A big hole in the ground.
A big lock on the gate.
A big hulk carrying a big sword
who would like nothing better
than to leave a big empty space above my shoulders.

I've hit the big times all right, God,
and You've blessed me every step.
Are You listening, God?
That's a joke.
Are You laughing?
I'm laughing.
It's a scream!

I'm falling out of my chair . . .
Oh, it's not a chair . . .
It's a stone bench
in a stone dungeon

about four levels deeper than the sun ever reaches.
A good place for a belly laugh.

Are You having a belly laugh, God?

It hurts.
It hurts so bad.
I don't understand it,
not any of it.
But if You're not still God
there's nothing left.

O God, how long?

Photo by Brian Austin [3]

Brian Austin

Youth Ministry

Forty teens worshipping.
Another twenty,
not sure they are ready for worship,
free to be close
without compulsion to be involved.
Risky freedom many would think.

Leaders ready to accept kids as they are,
whether they fit the "church mold" or not.
Someone in tears drawn with a touch,
a hug, a gentle smile,
a listening ear,
a little prayer huddle.

A parent who loves teens
but appreciates small doses
watches with wonder and thankfulness.

Unseen by human eyes
unheard by human ears
God applauds!

Youth Ministry
The Gates of Hell Tremble Before It!

BLAMING GOD

I wished not to understand that I must reap what I had sown –
the bad as well as the good.

I used to rail against God. I used to cry out:
"Why is there still a problem?
Why do these habits still haunt me?
I've asked for forgiveness.
I've asked for cleansing.
Are Your promises not true?"

In some secret place of my heart
He not so much spoke
as painted a word-picture.

In a garden, I saw a father's hand
around a child's, pulling up weeds.
I saw the two of them
gazing through a microscope.

He turned my thoughts to the past.
On the screen of my mind, He brought images.
Most were pleasant and fine;
a father and child together in the garden.

But two or three brief scenes
showed the child alone;
the father at a distance, watching.
The child was tearing out weeds,
shaking defiant fists in the direction
he *thought* the father was,
scattering weed seeds,
grinding them into the dirt with his heel.

Brian Austin

Those scenes were followed – always
by a soiled, tear-stained face
drawn into the father's loving arms.

I used to rail against God.
I used to loudly complain.
But we pulled a weed together,
His hand over mine.
We placed the rotting seed husk
under a microscope.

I used to rail against God.
I used to question His love.
I could not understand
why habits of sin still plagued me.
Then he turned my gaze to the microscope.
It was *My Fingerprints* on the weed seed.

Grief crushed my spirit.
I was too unworthy for His love.
It was unthinkable that He should pull weeds
I had planted.

In foolish pride, I scorned tears.
I tried to pretend it did not matter.
But once, as together we pulled weeds
a tear splashed on my arm.
Startled, I looked in His face.
Love shone there!

On the screen of my mind,
more pictures played.
I saw a weed-infested garden,
the boundaries clearly marked.

A few splashes of colour
hinted of flowers among the tangle.
Then – with what wonder?
I saw within those same boundaries
blossoms of rare beauty,
fragrance and colour
drawing bees and hummingbirds.

There were still weeds, but they were few.
The garden was not yet all it would become.
But compared with the tangled mess
of a not-so-distant yesterday,
it was a place of beauty and rest.

I used to rail against God.
But once,
as His hand covered mine
while together we pulled
a weed of my planting,
I saw the scars.
A thorn – or something worse
had pierced Him through.
Fresh blood welled from the wound.

I could not help myself.
As tears streamed down my face
I clutched that bloody hand
against my breast
and wept.

Love,
measured in hours of patient labor;
Love,
measured in crimson drops...

The blood-stain of His love marks me.
It is His trademark
on every blossom.

I used to rail against God.
Sometimes,
child that I am
I still do.
But He's still in the garden,
laboring in love,
hands covering mine.

I used to rail against God.
But now,
as people walk through the garden
I long for the message to be clear
that 'tis *Him* has made the difference
and *Here Love Dwells!*

The Undaunted

The barometer is falling
but her proud bow cleanly breasts the waves.
Strong the current - and the winds oppose.
She shivers, then, like a colt newly released
seems to leap.

Her crew stand firm to their posts
though their Captain has moved on
and the First Officer is ill ashore.
At the helm is one who knows with intimacy
this ship and all her moods.
Not yet has the new Captain walked her decks,
put her through her paces,
sought to know her like a lover.

In the engine room the smell of oil
perfumes the gleaming metal
while a deep, growling purr whispers, "All is well."

Ere the captain left the ship, the pumps were inspected.
Seams were checked, rigging and rudder examined.
Pronounced sea-worthy she was,
and sound from bow to stern.

Brian Austin

A sturdy ship, though not so big
as some that ply these waters.
Clean her lines, though not so elegant as some,
for a working vessel she is,
not some millionaire's plaything.
Storm clouds loom and thunder grumbles.
A seam begins to leak.
The waves beat harder.
The wind howls and shrieks.

Rain drives like bullets.
The crew batten down the hatches.
Water pours from her scuppers.
She leans against the wind
as waves break across her deck.

A rogue wave strikes and she shudders.
Passengers, with mingled thrill and fear line the glass
gasping with wonder -
For few the sights more noble
than a proud ship
with its bow in the teeth of a storm.

Yet another seam begins to leak.
The waves beat with hammer blows.
The engine noise growls deeper.
The hands at the helm grip tighter.
Furtive glances pass among the crew.

According to their nature,
passengers delight or cower.

The pumps engage as more seams leak
and waves continue to batter.

A cable breaks.
A slender pole of steel falls.
The lifeboats - meager security enough
lie dashed and shattered.

The hand at the helm does not falter,
though the knuckles show white.

Hands that know hard work,
but not this task are offered;
hands unskilled for this moment's need.

Yet trust in the crew is voiced,
and love for the ship.
Not blind trust - but earned.
Not shallow love, though its strength has ne'er been tested.

One takes his place at a pump that labors and complains.
Lies on his belly in the bilge water
clearing the intake,
listening to the pump's voice change.

Brian Austin

Pride swells as he sees others
with skills no bigger than his own
offering what they have.
The waves hit gentler now,
though the seams are leaking fast.
Barely can the pumps keep pace.

But pails and lids and even caps
bail water.
Rags stuff seams.

Skilled and unskilled,
side by side share their fear, their love and their trust
as the storm makes a wide circle
and begins to approach again.

And the ship,
proud ship
undaunted - faces the waves.

Checking Out Hell

I checked out Hell the other day.
It wasn't all that great.
The recruitment team was absent.
No greeters at the gate.

I could hear the wail of haunted souls
but no one could I see.
The only company I had
were memories and me.

Just memories of foolish words
and selfish, cruel tricks;
of hateful, vengeful, twisted pride
getting in a few more kicks.

Memories of love offered,
but scorned and spit upon,
of opportunities that come but once,
and now forever gone.

Memories of things I could have done
but ignored with nose held high
while I chose the willful worship
of the mighty god of "I."

I woke in sweat-stained, twisted bed
with covers in a knot.
Cried out to God for one more chance
to change my eternal lot.

All eternity, to reap rewards
of worshiping the god of "I."
I could not bear to contemplate.
I could only groan and cry.

God met me there with smiling face,
not the judgment I deserved.
He covered me with love and grace.
A new place He reserved.

For Hell to which my lifestyle led
He paid the outstanding fee.
Because of Him, and *only* Him
today I'm fully free.

Day of Darkness

Two pictures does the Bible paint
of a single point in time:
one of hopelessness and shame,
one of joy sublime.

Two pictures does the church embrace
in its language and its creed:
one of a world destined for Hell,
one, Heav'n meeting each need.

As part of the church I've wondered oft'
how it can be that I
so little care which path you choose,
if you live or if you die.

If the bridge was washed out on our road
you can bet I'd flag you down,
stand in your path, force you to swerve
rather than let you drown.

I'd take the risk that you might not stop,
put myself in danger's way
nor think that was too big a price
from death your path to sway.

But to make a nuisance of myself,
to meddle in your life
when it's only Hell, not a broken bridge . . .
well – it might cause you strife.

And I'm told I'm not supposed to judge
or try to interfere.
It's not *"correct"* to push beliefs
or fill your thoughts with fear.

So I hide behind what's deemed *"correct"*
as you breeze your way to Hell.
I hoard the message of the Book.
If you ask, I s'pose I'll tell . . .

The words of hope within it found;
the message of God's love;
the payment that for you was made
the home prepared above.

But if the bridge was washed out on our road,
I wouldn't wait for you to ask.
To warn you of the danger there
would be my highest task.

Two pictures does the Bible paint
of a single point in time:
one of hopelessness and shame,
one of joy sublime.

And I claim it's God's revealed Word
and attest that it is true.
Just maybe that implies something
that I should share with you.

Just maybe, Hell's a greater risk
than a washout on life's way.
So if I care, I'll flag you down
from Hell, your path to sway.

Perhaps you'll choose to run me down
mock my faith, call it fake.
But if I believe what I claim I do
that's a risk I'll have to take.

March 2003

Brian Austin

Where God Works

Not confined by
stained-glass windows,
not bound by
candlelight,

God's love reaches
lonely places,
shares the darkness
of soul's plight.

In The Storm

Lost – with Jesus in the boat.
Terrified – with the creator only steps away.
Blind – with the light of the world beside them.
Confused – with the truth close enough to touch.

Tis a strange tale, and a troubling,
Jesus sleeping in the storm
while His followers – closest friends – battle with fears.

And I? Had I been in that boat –
would my courage have been greater?
The Big Fisherman – Peter – he knew the storms of Galilee.
If *he* feared – big and brash and bold –
would my land-locked knees have held me straight and tall!?

Lost – with my Saviour just a breath away.
Terrified – yet the One who spoke the world into existence
has counted the hairs of my head – not so big a task as it once was.
He knows when every sparrow falls.
He is the Resurrection and the Life.
He walked the road to the cross in love for me.

And yet I doubt.

When the storm hits, I cower and cry out in fear.
I tremble and my knees grow weak.

But like a father, His hand covers mine
and suddenly I'm bold enough to face a lion.
The storm frightens me no more.

But – my hands grow numb with the cold rain.
I cannot feel His touch.
My eyes are blinded by the spray.
I cannot see His face.
Again, I doubt.
The noise of the storm fills my senses.
I cannot hear His voice.

Lost – with Jesus beside me in the storm.
Terrified – with the creator only steps away.
Blind – with the light of the world beside me.
Confused – with the truth close enough to touch.

His only rebuke – "Why did you doubt?"
The light of love in His eyes.
The touch of His hand on my shoulder.
Even the winds and the waves obey Him.
There in the storm I kneel
and own Him, LORD.

> **Homeless Trilogy**
>
> These three poems were written during cold February days to explore the pain and frustration of being homeless. The theme of a ventilation grate, giving barely enough warmth to maintain life, appears is all three.

A Bed of Roses

Welcome to the great-room of my palatial home
where I watch from my grate, like a king from his throne
as the traffic rumbles from dusk to dawn,
people rushing to nowhere – each one a pawn
in a frantic game where there are no rules
and the busiest ones are the biggest fools.

Well – I'm not too busy – as I sit on this grate
and watch the masses chasing fate.
Though the wind finds the cracks in the castle walls
and cuts like a knife down these old, wide halls.
And the sky is my roof and it sometimes leaks
and I haven't been truly warm in weeks.

It's an old, old castle – and the dining room
is the dumpster deli – behind *The Spoon.*
And the chef is a pro and the smells of heaven
reach to a man by hunger driven.
Now the menu's not all that I might choose
and I've thought of firing him – What would I lose?

Brian Austin

For he curses when he sees me – though I am king
of the street and the grate, and this mess we're in.
And I give my orders as the traffic roars
and I get the finger and I get the stares.
But that's all right – for I "own" this grate
with its stingy warmth – that I love to hate.

It's warmth scarce enough to maintain life
but it won't let me die and end the strife.
So I'll sit on this grate – like a king on his throne
as you chase your dreams to work and home.
And I might dream too – though I am king
for it's not all roses – this bed I'm in.

Photo by Alanna Rusnak. [2]

Homeless?

Disappointment on disappointment
as lifelong dreams decay and rust.
The ashes of a life of promise
paint mocking memories – fade to dust.

The wind that knifes through my thin jacket
brings stinging tears upon my cheek.
To cry would bring a twisted pleasure
weeping for the things I seek.

But strength is needed for surviving
while losses mourned keep piling up.
And strong I've grown through life's abuses.
I'll laugh to drink this bitter cup.

Although the why of my surviving
raises questions – no answers given.
So mocks my mind with bitter laughter
and calls this rusty steel – Heaven.

For rising from the grate beneath me
a meager warmth, grudging supply.
This hard-edged steel defines my prison,
fails to give life – nor lets me die.

While memories of some far-past lifetime . . .
a wedding ring – a bed to share
Softer. Warmer. Passion. Laughter.
Someone to love. Someone to care.

Just mocks the hateful, vengeful present
as with empty belly I smell a feast
and count the hours until the dumpster
draws me like some gutter-beast . . .

To a meal I blush to speak of.
You'd think of pride I'd have none left.
This is my home! Come! Share my riches!
We'll toast a world of hope bereft.

Photo by Alanna Rusnak [2]

Laughter & Tears

The Ventilation Grate

Ah, just a glimpse, the briefest glimpse
of a face that I once knew,
and the gentle touch of a loving hand
would be enough to see me through . . .

This night as cold as the heart of Hell
and as lonely as the grave
as I crouch here on this steel grate,
to its grudging warmth – a slave.

And the memories mock and the traffic roars
and the crowds walk blindly by
as I curse the warmth that gives no life
but still won't let me die.

Ha!

Did you know I held a job once?
And walked with head held high?
And dreamed my dreams and chased my goals
with sights set on the sky?

Did you know I wore a wedding ring
in some lifetime long ago?
And shared a bed with its wonders warm
and my spirit all aglow?

Brian Austin

And I drove a Thunderbird once
and I gazed with boastful scorn
on an old gray-beard – on this very grate
and I blasted with the horn.

And I rolled my window down once
and I shouted, *"Get a job!"*
And I felt disgust as he chewed a crust
from the gutter – like a dog.

But the old gray-beard is gone now.
Another fills his place.
And the grate gives stingy, meager warmth
to another in disgrace.

And the mocking hasn't changed much
though I hear it with new ears.
The joke's lost all its laughter.
I'm the target of the jeers.

And I haven't seen that face now
and I haven't felt that touch
of a loving hand with gentle warmth
that I long for – O so much.

And the memories mock and the traffic roars
and the crowds walk blindly by
as I curse the warmth that gives no life,
but still won't let me die.

No Room For Tears

The tears don't come anymore.
He just walks the street.
His little feet stumble
as he searches for a place to sleep
in some cold doorway.

The rags he wears for clothes
are vile with dirt
and they give no warmth
as he crouches in a dark corner.

His hands, though occupied a short time ago,
are empty.
The old worn rag doll,
his only token of love
was taken by a gang of boys
and ripped apart.

Now he huddles,
cold and empty,
alone.
but the tears don't come.

Brian Austin

A Cup of Cool Water

Just a cup of cool water;
an act of kindness, small
through the hours of a long and weary day.
No fanfare with the giving.
No trumpet call or blazing lights.
Prob'ly embarrassed by the thanks I'd like to say.

T'was a gift received with gratefulness.
Did I even speak the words?
You couldn't know the value of your gift.
My weary spirit freshened.
I was tired to the bone
but through your kind act, I felt my spirit lift.

So let me whisper, thank you.
Your timing was just right.
Your "little" gift gave O - so much to me.
May God reward you richly
for a kindness you thought small,
for the Christ-likeness in you that I see.[4]

Laughter & Tears

For Grieving Hearts

Blessed are they that mourn For they shall be Comforted

Matthew 5:4 KJV

Photo by Brian Austin [3]

Brian Austin

Forever

Tiny breast still. Gone the tremor of life.
Just a pale ashen face in the swirling snow.
Blue lips parted in a still, peaceful smile.
Eyes closed, sealed by frozen tears.
Soft in the howl of the wind.
Peaceful 'gainst the driven snow.
Just a child, all alone,
and no life remains.
But the smile on her lips is forever.

Laughter & Tears

Dylan

They sneak up without warning,
these hot and painful tears.
They squeeze the chest and crush the will.
They do not still the fears . . .

That torture – though the worst
has already taken place.
A little one so longed for
has hid from us his face.

So great was our rejoicing!
Was it so few days ago
when the coming of this little one
set our hearts aglow?

Parents, loved ones, grandparents,
we joyed to speak his name;
treasured the glimpses of each day;
spread abroad his fame;

Longed for the chance to hold him;
spoke his name with deep delight;
were sure the world was brighter
'neath the glow of his small light.

But he's gone now and we're aching
with the great unanswered why
God loans a child for so few days
then lets that child die.

Brian Austin

*Not the first to feel such sorrow;
we will not be the last.
But this pain is ours – so bottomless.
Seems it will forever last.*

*But God shares in our sorrows;
knows how deep a loved one grieves;
saw His loved and cherished Son die,
hung between two thieves.*

*And He does not let a tear fall
where He does not share the pain.
And He sees beyond our present grief
to when we'll meet again.*

*Tis a promise that we treasure
though the tears still fall today.
God holds our precious little one
to reunite with us one day.*

*And the tears, so deep and painful
cannot outreach His love.
So we'll trust our precious little one
in the hands of God above.* [5]

Photo by Jason Edgcumbe [1]

The Weariness of Sorrow

There's a weariness in sorrow
that drains my strength away.
I'm too exhausted to go on
half way through the day.

Yet my mind will not grow quiet
as I lie in bed at night.
It tries to play the *what if* game
from sundown until light.

But in God I find refuge
deeper than the painful *why's*.
I'll trust Him, though the whole world
should claim I'm trusting lies.

For in the midst of sorrow
there is peace and rest and love.
I know that my Redeemer lives
and ever reigns above.

I know He's shared this sorrow
and others deeper still.
I'll trust Him through the painful days
and lean upon His will.

There's a weariness in sorrow
and my strength seems far too small,
but God is close beside me,
upholding, lest I fall.

Brian Austin

There's a weariness in sorrow,
but God shares all my pain.
I'm resting in His goodness
and rejoicing once again.

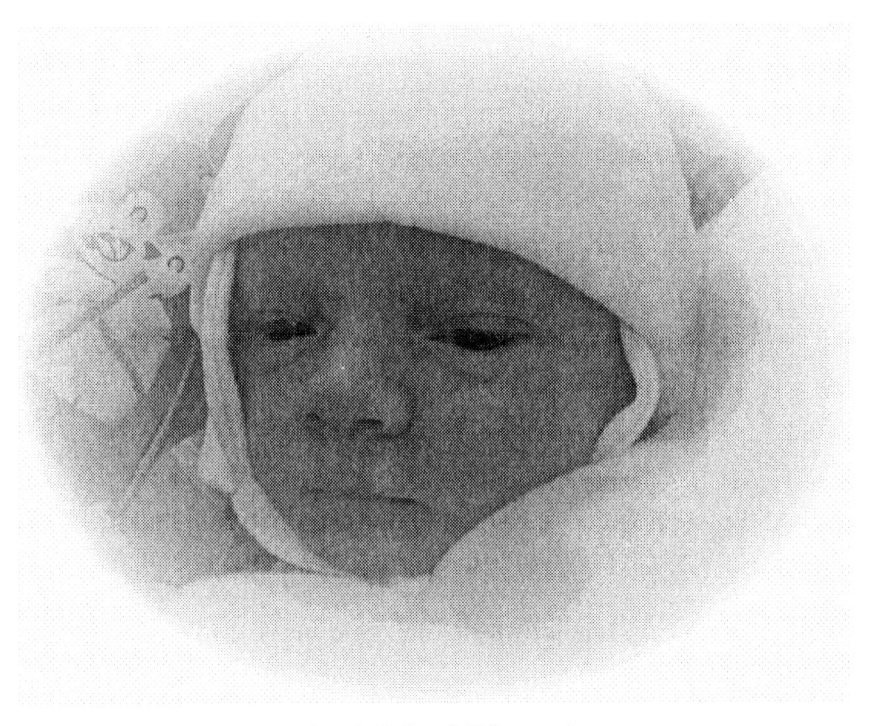

Dylan Michael Edgcumbe
March 3, 2003 to March 8, 2003

Photo by Jason Edgcumbe [1]

Laughter & Tears

Farewell, Little One

To see your tiny form in the casket softly lie,
The glowing redness of your cheek, your closed and sleeping eye,

And to ache so deep to hold you, press your cheek against my face,
To whisper a grandparent's love with an oh, so tight embrace . . .

Yet giv'n so very carefully, that it might not do you harm;
To feel the weight of a little one nestled in my arm;

To see a daughter's tear-stained face, son's shoulders bowed with grief,
To have no words that comfort brings, no source of quick relief;

To say goodbye, before we've had a chance to say hello,
To lay you in the cold, cold earth, cover your cheek's red glow;

Ah, grief! I thought I knew before something of its pain.
Yet through the tears I know that God will let us meet again.

And though we cry a river, and our tears will mingled flow,
we know you're held in loving arms, and Heaven's all aglow.

So farewell, precious little one, held in the arms of God.
We know that it's not really you we've laid beneath the sod.

You're celebrating in a world made perfect in every way.
And we'll wait with eager longing to join you there one day.

Brian Austin

In the Darkest Hour

*Staring at the ceiling as the moments creep away.
Longing for the night to pass, but dreading a new day.
Exhausted, but unsleeping, with itching, burning eyes,
painting mindless pictures on the darkened ceiling tiles.*

*Yet knowing God's love has not changed,
nor dimmed, nor taken flight,
knowing that above the clouds the sun is shining bright,
I'll dare to hope though hope seems dead; a mindless fool's creed,
and faith has shriveled smaller than a tiny mustard seed.*

*For God has promised. In the past He's always kept His Word.
Him I'll trust, though feelings say trusting is absurd.
And though the storm clouds blind my eyes to sun shining above,
the day will come – pray it be soon – when I feel again His love.* [6]

Photo by Brian Austin [3]

Laughter & Tears

09/11/2001 Grief

In sorrow deep o'er wasted death,
I have grieved for hours today.
So many lives with their hopes and dreams,
callously swept away.
I've cried those scalding, male-choked tears
that are trained to never fall,
but break the rules on days like this.
Leave me no pride at all.

Sickness deep has gripped my frame,
and crushed me to the core.
I believe in life, but I've stared at death.
I'm sure I'll cry still more.
Who understands the minds of
men and women who can do
such wretched deeds, and make such plans,
and follow those plans through?

Grief and anger, sickness, rage,
surge through me like a flood.
On the screen I see streets choked
with ashes, bodies, blood.
Were they worse sinners than I am?
Why should they have to die?
Don't spout a pious, "it's God's will."
I'll tell you, "that's a lie!"

God is not behind such deeds.
They were not planned above.
He records the tears of those who weep.
He shares their pain in love.
And He has the power, so hard to grasp,
from tragedy to bring,
good where good we cannot see.
Once more will people sing.

And because He holds eternity
within His firm control,
He offers comfort to those who grieve,
e'en while their tears still flow.
So Him I'll trust. On Him I'll lean,
while my heart is rocked with pain.
It may not be soon, but the day will come,
when I wish to sing again.

In sorrow deep o'er wasted death,
I have grieved for hours today.
I'm too far away for rescue work,
but I'm not too far to pray.
Though I have no answers for the questions
raging in my mind
I'll lift your grieving soul to God,
who is loving, great and kind. [7]

Shared Tears

When wounds are deeper than words can heal;
when you've plumbed the pit of pain;
when you can't imagine the day will come
that you might smile again;
When you hurt with a bottomless depth of hurt,
more than you believed you could endure
and it seems that life has nothing left
and death's the only cure;

*Then let me cry with you awhile,
share aching, silent tears.
Lean on me. Accept a hug.
Let me bear some of your fears.
I can't undo the hurt you feel
or take away your pain.
I can't bring back what you have lost
or make you whole again.
But if I'm wise enough to silent be
and only share my tears,
t'will be greater gift than wondrous words
with wisdom of the years.*

When the night has dragged a century long
but you dread the coming day.
When your tears are wrung out, stale and dry
but the pain won't go away.
When you're all alone in a private hell
but voices try to force an in
and you're empty, hollow, sick and numb;
just a deadening ache within;

Brian Austin

Then let me cry with you awhile,
share aching, silent tears.
Lean on me. Accept a hug.
Let me bear some of your fears.
I can't undo the hurt you feel
or take away your pain.
I can't bring back what you have lost
or make you whole again.
But if I'm wise enough to silent be
and only share my tears,
t'will be greater gift than wondrous words
with wisdom of the years.

When one you love has let you down
and you're wounded through and through.
When they've gone away in a final way
and the healing's left to you.
When your living heart from beneath your breast
has been crushed and ripped apart;
When your eyes are dry, no tears left to cry,
just a wound where you had a heart;

Then let me cry with you awhile,
share aching, silent tears.
Lean on me. Accept a hug.
Let me bear some of your fears.
I can't undo the hurt you feel
or take away your pain.
I can't bring back what you have lost
or make you whole again.
But if I'm wise enough to silent be
and only share my tears,
t'will be greater gift than wondrous words
with wisdom of the years.

Laughter & Tears

When everyone has a word to share
and their words are prob'ly true;
but your wounds are just too deep to care
and it's all just noise to you;
When you're dead inside and you want to hide
but life demands you play your role;
when the Love of God is lost in a fog;
just surviving seems a hopeless goal;

Then let me cry with you awhile,
share aching, silent tears.
Lean on me. Accept a hug.
Let me bear some of your fears.
I can't undo the hurt you feel
or take away your pain.
I can't bring back what you have lost
or make you whole again.
But if I'm wise enough to silent be
and only share my tears,
t'will be greater gift than wondrous words
with wisdom of the years. [8]

Photo by Brian Austin [3]

Brian Austin

The Echo of My Weeping

So empty - my words of wisdom.
So shallow - the comfort of my pen.
A poet's skill and talent turned to the task
fails!
Shared tears . . .
Shared tears alone speak a deeper language.

Not the myth of understanding.
Not even the *"I've been there"* line
though truth there might be in those words.

So be still my pen.
Spill no more ink on paper
except as tears smudge the print.
Speak no more words with those who grieve
except as the echo of your weeping
speaks the deeper language
of shared tears. [9]

I Faced a Man

It is raining; little more than a cold drizzle. For four days we have fought in this sullen atmosphere, with the smell of gunpowder and smoke, and the sound of guns in the air.

Yesterday, across a little clearing, with the grass charred and scorched, I faced a man.

There was no hesitation on the part of either of us. One of his bullets grazed my side. Four rounds from my gun smashed his chest. He died almost instantly.

He was my "enemy." This is war. But I am sorry.

I have killed – how many times now? Still I am sick each time.

I am sorry. How empty those words sound. I wish there was something I could say or do, but there is nothing.

The letters he was carrying from you I am returning. I hope that in some small way they will lessen the grief.

There was a picture – he carried over his heart. Most of that picture, he now carries within his body. You have lost him, but he has not lost you.

I laid him under the trees where the grass was still green and no shells had scorched and destroyed. His rifle and helmet mark the spot.

The fighting is getting intense again. I dare not stay, or even carry this letter with me. I hope somehow, it gets to you.

I am sorry.

From a man who in better days would have shared a cup of coffee with the one I just killed.

Brian Austin

Unwanted

He was a man nobody wanted.
He was a boy with no tears left to cry.
He was called garbage.
He was called trash.
Hunted down like a dog
he was jailed,
then condemned to die.
At his execution
he asked for mercy
from the One who looked
most powerless to help.

The words of Jesus:

"Today you will be with me in paradise."

Even for the Damned

No stained glass windows in this place.
Hope's a forgotten dream.
We curse and swear as we prowl our lair,
and in our sleep we scream.

There's a chapel in this hellish place
and the music sometimes leaks
'tween the cold steel bars and the guard's hard stares
to us lifers and deadbeats.
And we laugh the laugh of the damned, because –
those songs are not for us.
We've won the label of scum of the earth –
so preacher, save your fuss.

It's Christmas Eve and they're singing now –
God's love and peace on earth.
God's love in this trophy to hate and crime,
where devil's schemes come to birth?
The bars were forged in a place of fire;
twisted, bent by hate.
There's only one way out for us –
through death's cruel beckoning gate.

But there's a baby's cry and a woman's voice,
at the heart of this man-made hell
and the memory of a story my mother told
penetrates my stinking cell.

Brian Austin

The woman stops her singing;
tries to hush her little one.
I'm crying, and can't seem to stop
as I remember a long lost son;
And a family I loved, when I once knew how –
a family who once loved me,
but I haven't seen for years because
I chose a path I thought was free.
The preacher is talking about a rigged up trial
with a mob that loved to hate.
He's mixing the baby story with Easter stuff,
and I'm trying to relate.

He's talking of a thief on his way to Hell
who received an answer kind
from the man on the middle cross
who was dying too, but still had time to mind
the prayer of a guy who didn't know how
a man was supposed to pray
so just blurted out the words that came
as they both hung there that day.

And I'm feeling something I haven't felt
since I don't remember when,
like someone could love this wasted life
and want me back again.
I wipe my tears and shake the bars.
I want to break the preacher's head.
But I want to believe what he says is true.
Someone cares that I'm not dead.

There's a chapel in this hellish place.
Tonight a baby cries.
A woman sings and her soft voice wings
to a heart that has fed on lies.

Eyes that can laugh in the face of death
are wet with streaming tears
and I'm holding fiercely to the bit of hope
that has reached beyond my fears.

Brian Austin

Celebrating

the Coming

B. Austin [3]

Grumpy Santa

Santa Claus is grumpy.
His cell-phone battery's dead.
The reindeer are on strike for sweeter hay.
The elves threw quite a party.
The punch was mixed by Jed.
Their headaches threaten Christmas Day.

The toy factory is humming
but power rates are up.
Not e'en a North-Pole address gets a break.
Santa's worn down to a shadow.
Look in the mirror brings a sigh.
Anyone sees him will think he's fake.

Rudolf has the sniffles.
His nose is sore and red.
He says there's too much weight in Santa's sleigh.
He's been clicking on his website.
He *won't* stay put in bed.
Trying to streamline that old sleigh in every way.

Jed is making eggnog.
Santa's dumping it on the sly,
but it's melting through the snow and permafrost.
Dancer's working a new waltz.
Dasher's on the fly.
Comet claims his tail has been lost.

Mrs. Claus has had enough.
Santa's sleeping on the couch.
Makes his grouching worse, 'cause now his toes are cold.
Cupid's into archery.
Elves keep saying "Ouch!"
Romantic notions are making shy guys bold.

The computer has a virus.
Rudolf has a cold.
The toy factory is sinking in a hole.
The smell of eggnog's rising,
with rum's sweet odour bold.
Santa's threatening the elves with bags of coal.

Santa Claus is grumpy,
but Christmas is on time,
and bringing joy gives joy to givers too.
So Santa will be beaming
time the sleigh's parked one more time,
and dreaming of next season's work to do.

Love Revealed

I'd draw a picture if I could
of One who had great skill with wood;
of One who learned the carpenter's trade,
though by His Word, whole worlds were made.

I'd draw a stable - crude and bare.
Seems strange God's Son should be born there;
that He who formed the universe
should lie in manger after birth.

A cattle stall for a king?
Yet it was here the songs did ring
as angels sang the Saviour's birth;
God's love revealed - 'Peace on Earth.'

Behind the stable I'd draw a cross;
a scene of hate - and death - and loss.
Its shadow o'er the babe would fall
and form the sword piercing Mary's soul.

Behind the cross, an empty tomb,
No longer filled with death and gloom.
Beside it stands the Risen King!!
Now angels songs again do ring.

Peace on Earth comes at awesome cost.
The babe was born to face the cross.
Christmas is God's love revealed.
The shed blood is sin's curse repealed.

I cannot look on manger scene
without asking, "What does it mean?"
Love poured out for you and me
is defined in stable and Calvary's tree. [10]

Photo by Brian Austin. [3]

Laughter & Tears

No Vacancy
The retelling of an old, old story

The *No Vacancy* sign was glowing,
the lobby locked and dark.
Her contractions coming three minutes apart.
The gas gauge sat on empty.
The wipers squeaked and hissed.
Her eyes betrayed the aching of her heart.

A power saw in the back seat,
hammers, levels, planes;
the tools of her husband's stock and trade.
Work-worn hands could build a cabinet
with an artist's fine honed skill.
But tonight he just couldn't make the grade.

He barely stopped the tremble
of calloused, aching hands
as they gripped the steering wheel with crushing force.
Capable of so many things
helpless now he sat.
He could not alter the coming baby's course.

Her contractions coming faster . . .
The tears pushed past her eyes
He raised his gaze in silent, pleading prayer.
Unused was he to terror,
to helplessness and shame;
unused to no resources left but prayer.

Brian Austin

The car door slammed behind him.
Through the sleet and freezing rain
to the riding stable tucked back of the Inn
He didn't know if he was searching
or just running away.
He felt his helplessness the blackest sin.

The horse smell struck him strongly
as the barn door hinges groaned.
It was a warm, but strong and earthy smell.
A single light-bulb glimmered.
The horses stamped within.
For his bride and baby . . .? It seemed a kind of hell.

But desperation can with little
do much when there is need.
Clean straw in a corner there was piled.
He felt himself a failure,
but t'was the best that he could do
for shelter for his wife and coming child.

A small bag she had ready
with blankets, diapers, clothes.
She sank into the straw with weary sigh.
And long before the morning,
with her husband kneeling close,
in that horse-barn came an infant's cry.

The *No Vacancy* sign was glowing,
the lobby locked and dark,
but a healthy baby boy was born that night.
Her husband felt a failure,
yet it seemed that angels sang
and that old barn glowed with brighter light.

The gas gauge sat on empty.
Their savings were all gone.
The rusty car was clothed in crystal white.
Snow was falling thickly
when a knock came at the door.
Some neighbours had struggled through the night.

They told a tale unlikely,
more like a drunken dream,
but their breath betrayed no hint of beer or wine.
Gazed with wonder on the baby,
left simple, little gifts;
Praised God for His rich gift. Called it fine.

The *No Vacancy* sign was glowing.
The snow was falling fast.
The morning sun was just a feeble glow.
A baby pressed to mother's breast
drew sustenance and warmth.
Love overflowed that barn, so white with snow. [11]

Brian Austin

On a Lighter Note

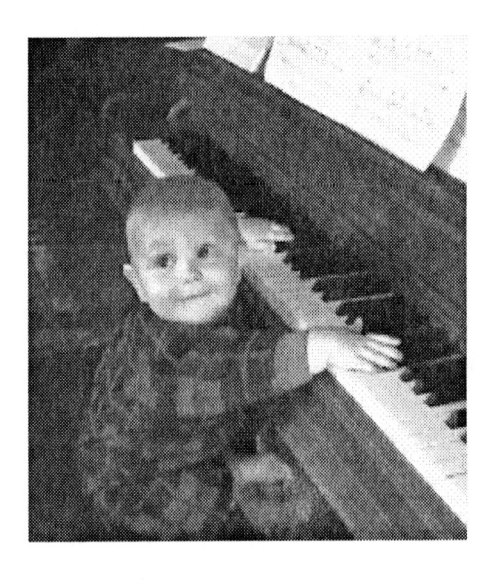

Photo by Alanna Rusnak. [2]

Laughter & Tears

Eye Teeth

I went to the eye doctor who looked at my eye teeth.
He sent me to the dentist to get me some relief.
The dentist gave me glasses. It's awful as can be,
cause I'm seeing half-chewed pizza now, all mixed up with my tea.

I went to the shoe store to fix my smelly feet.
They gave me a big clothes-pin. Said it the smell would beat.
I cannot smell a thing now but my nose is sore and red
and my little sister laughs at me before she goes to bed.

I went to the farmer, a chocolate shake to buy.
He sent me out to Bessy and I looked her in the eye.
I asked her most politely, but she showed me her backside
then kicked me into next week and I think I must have died.

Now I hadn't ever died before so I may have done things wrong
'cause I woke up in the middle of a mournful funeral song
in a box all white and frilly, with a clothespin by my head
and bagpipes loudly playing the Requiem for the Dead.

Don't like to criticize the music – but it wasn't quite my style
so I jumped the box and headed straight down the church's aisle.
The bagpipes gave a dying squawk. Piper stared at me with dread.
I guess he'd never quite believed his song could raise the dead.

The preacher had been warming to a resurrection theme
but his face – it turned a most peculiar shade of green.
Now my eye-teeth, thanks to Bessy, and the glasses too are gone
and I really didn't want to hear another funeral song.

Brian Austin

It seemed I was disturbing them, though why I couldn't tell.
The eye-doctor was in the crowd so I thought it just as well
to put a bit of distance 'tween myself and that strange bunch,
though it was a fancy funeral with a really fancy lunch.

But since Bessy'd knocked my teeth out
I'd have to eat it through a straw
with the added inconvenience of a badly aching jaw.
Grabbed a paper. Read my obit as I left town on the tear.
Sprayed graffiti on my way out, "Of Eye-Doctors – Beware."

> **The Meddling Trilogy**
>
> Tampering without apology where wiser people would keep silent.

The Weed

She sported a soft smile beautiful.
She drew second looks from the guys.
Her skin was flawless. Her lips were full.
Her form delighted the eyes.

She took great pains with personal care.
She wore just a hint of perfume.
She carried herself with poise and flare.
She could almost make grown men swoon.

Soft spoken but fun, she would flash that smile.
Young men's hearts all around would stop.
Just one minor flaw. T'was a *little* thing.
Stale tobacco stink clung like rot.

She was a true beauty, in the fairest sense
in body and spirit and style.
A delight to be near, and I mean no offence,
from a few yards away I would smile.

But the smell of the weed that clung to her
if she came within range of my nose
was worse than the stink of my sweaty shoes
when athlete's foot itched my toes.

Brian Austin

She'd have never considered heading to school
with her hair in a tangled mess.
Her complexion was clear. Her demeanor was cool.
She showed taste in her style of dress.

And if I'd been young and single again
she'd have giv'n my heart a bad time.
But the tobacco smoke was a bad, bad joke
like a poem that just wouldn't rhyme.

So I wonder if it's really worth the cost
to purse-strings and health and all
to smell like you've burned in the garbage heap
when boys start coming to call.

I'll probably not know, 'cause I'm an old man
in the books of my daughters three.
But the smell of stale smoke is a bad, bad joke.
On that, we all agree.

The Hunk

He winked and flexed his muscles.
He was what you'd call a hunk.
But the truth of it, if you care to know,
and it's sad to say, "He Stunk!"

He was pretty pleased with what he saw
reflecting from the mirror.
When he made a girl blush bright red
he would grin from ear to ear.

He'd flash that handsome, wicked smile.
Female hearts would quake.
Squeals and panting whispers
would follow in his wake.

But when he managed to get close
to one who caught his eye,
it was like a cloud swept o'er her face.
She'd look like she might die.

He never could quite understand
why the ones who'd let him close
were often very beautiful
but they seemed to smell quite gross,

while the ones who smelled quite heavenly
would quickly back away.
When he tried to steal a little kiss
their faces would go gray.

And no one ever clued him in.
They thought it impolite.
But the stink of stale tobacco clung
like ghost of nightmare's fright.

And I suppose he is trying still
to win one special girl.
But when he breathes too close to her
she loses all the curl

in the hairdo she has just spent hours
trying to get just right.
She's not impressed and she lets him know
he can kiss his dreams good night.

So I wonder if it's worth the cost
of sucking one more time
on a cigarette that makes you smell
as inviting as swamp slime.

It's probably not for me to say.
Passing judgment is uncool.
But paying to stink and ruin health
hints of actions of a fool.

Hell's Laughter

I look outside the high-school doors.
Nineteen is the age
at which it's permitted to play the fool,
suck on this weed that's all the rage.

Not one in fifty has passed that mark
from the timing of their birth.
How the marketers of death must laugh,
counting dollars in their mirth.

Just kids, just trying to be cool,
though each one knows the truth.
Just following the lead of movie stars,
feeling mighty in their youth.

Blind to the costs that the years will bring.
Blind to the clinging chains.
Mocking the toothless laws that guard
the hypocrisy of adult claims.

For the signs all say that it can't be bought
but their money fills the till.
The integrity of the adult world is rot.
They lack the courage or the will

to stop the trade that brings them wealth,
though it comes at the price of lives
And they close their eyes, prattle empty words
and complain to husbands and wives.

More addictive e'en than heroin
is this cruel habit's curse.
It robs of health and forges chains
e'en as it robs the purse.

The roots of the nicotine habit
reach all the way to Hell
as the ones who try to break it
can all so clearly tell.

And I look outside the high-school doors.
Nineteen is the age
at which it's permitted to play the fool,
suck on this weed that's all the rage.

Not one in fifty has passed that mark
from the timing of their birth.
How the marketers of death must laugh,
counting dollars in their mirth.

The Last Goodbye

It called for major surgery.
The diagnosis was not good.
I tried to keep a bright outlook
because I knew I should.

The Doctor shook his head.
He offered little hope.
He suggested that I should sit down
while heavy words he spoke.

Internal organs in a mess.
A cancer it would seem.
Long life and health had been replaced
with just a wishful dream.

I pretended well that I was strong
but inside cried a lot.
It seemed unfair – a cruel trick.
I was careful, was I not?

I fear a funeral is coming.
I wish not to attend.
Should the box be closed? Should the grave be deep?
Or should I just pretend?

We've battled and we've struggled
through long hours of the night
as we've fought to make a story work
and get the words just right.

Brian Austin

And we've fought the way that lovers do
as we've argued for our way.
But one of us stares with empty face,
blank and cold and gray.

What words do I dare to use
when it's down to boom or bust?
My computer, on this sad, sad day
has finally bit the dust.

Nitroglycerin

I've got a bottle of nitro
in the pocket of my jeans.
I can't find any answers
on just what a fall means.

I'd rather not make headlines
from a "suicide" attack,
but what happens if I stumble
and this bottle takes a smack?

I've got a bottle of nitro
in the pocket of my pants.
It's s'posed to help my heart out
but what will be my chance . . .

If it blows me into orbit
and sets the house on fire?
A man-sized hole in the roof
might stir my spouse's ire.

I've got a bottle of nitro.
I'm walking dynamite,
But every time I stumble
It gives me quite a fright

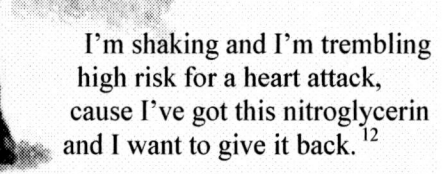

I'm shaking and I'm trembling
high risk for a heart attack,
cause I've got this nitroglycerin
and I want to give it back. [12]

Brian Austin

What's Growing in Your Clutter?

In the clutter and confusion
'neath papers, pencils, files
there's a poem growing silently
somewhere in all those piles.

And many a masterpiece has died
upon a cleaning day
when a writer clears his desktop
and throws the piles away.

So I'd rather not do murder
to some tiny growing verse,
that maturing might speak richer truth
or sound some quiet mirth . . .

At the foolishness of poets
and their pride in what they write
when it's grown there, slowly, silently
in the pile – while out of sight.

Alphabetical Index

Bed of Roses, A	40
Blaming God	24
Checking Out Hell	32
Coat of Faded Colours, A	20
Cup of Cool Water, A	47
Day of Darkness	34
Dylan	50
Echo of My Weeping, The	61
Even for the Damned	64
Eye Teeth	76
Farewell Little One	54
Forever	49
Grief	56
Grumpy Santa	68
Hell's Laughter	82
Homeless?	42
Hot, Hot Date, A	12
Hunk, The	80
I Faced a Man	62
In the Darkest Hour	55
In the Storm	38
Last Goodbye, The	84
Little Thing, A	9
Love Revealed	70
Mother's Love, A	6
Nitroglycerine	86
No Room for Tears	46
No Vacancy	72
Not for the Timid	10
Shared Tears	58
Susie's Beau	14
Table of Contents	ii
Tornado Lives at Our House, A	4
Undaunted, The	28
Unraveling, The	18

Unwanted	63
Ventilation Grate, The	44
Waiting Room, The	17
Weariness of Sorrow, The	52
Weed, The	78
What Is a Belly-Button For?	2
What's Growing In Your Clutter?	87
Where God Works	37
Youth Ministry	23

FIRST LINE INDEX

Ah, just a glimpse, the briefest glimpse, of a face	44
Disappointment on disappointment, as lifelong dreams	42
Forty teens worshiping. Another twenty, not sure they	23
He was a man nobody wanted	63
He winked and flexed his muscles. He was what	80
I checked out Hell the other day. It wasn't	32
I look outside the highs-school doors. Nineteen is	82
I used to rail against God. I used to cry out	24
I went to the eye-doctor who looked at my	76
I'd draw a picture if I could, of One who had great	70
I'm heading back to school again an' I just don't	14
In sorrow deep o'er wasted death, I have grieved	56
In the clutter and confusion, 'neath paper, pencils	87
It called for major surgery. The diagnosis was not	84
It is raining, little more than a cold drizzle. For four	62
It seemed to be so little to those who just looked on.	9
It's not a very pleasant room. It's small and	17
I've got a belly-button. I don't know what it's for.	2
I've got a bottle of nitro in the pocket of my jeans	86
Just a cup of cool water, an act of kindness	47
Lost – with Jesus in the boat. Terrified – with the	38
Love so oft' is stripped of all the strength behind	6
No stained glass windows in this place.	64
Not confined by stained-glass windows. Not bound	37
Not for the timid, yet what delight as you stretch	10

Laughter & Tears

Piling up the sleepless nights. So too the endless days 18
Santa Claus is grumpy. His cell phone battery's 68
She sported a soft smile beautiful. She drew 78
So empty, my words of wisdom. So shallow 61
Staring at the ceiling as the moments creep away 55
The barometer is falling, but her proud bow cleanly 28
The *No Vacancy* sign was glowing, the lobby 72
The tears don't come anymore. He just walks the 46
There lives a small tornado by the highway on the 4
There's a weariness in sorrow that drains my strength 52
They sneak up without warning, these hot 50
Tiny breast still, gone the tremor of life. Just 49
To see your tiny form in the casket softly lie 54
T'was a hot, hot date. She was young and sweet 12
Two pictures does the Bible paint of a single 34
Welcome to the great-room of my palatial home 40
When wounds are deeper than words can heal, ... 58
Why God? Were the dreams just a stupid 20

Endnotes

[1] Photographs by Jason Edgcumbe. Used by Permission. All Rights Reserved
[2] Photographs by Alanna Rusnak. Used by Permission. All Rights Reserved
[3] Photographs by Brian Austin. All Rights Reserved.
Note: all unlabeled Photographs and Clip-Art images are Royalty Free or in the Public Domain.
[4] *A Cup of Cool Water* Page 47 Published and sold as a *Greeting Card*.
[5] *Dylan* Page 50 Published and sold as a Greeting Card.
[6] *In the Darkest Hour* Page 55 Written September 9, 2001 – two days before the Terrorist Attack. Published in *The Durham Chronicle* September 2001. Published and sold as a *Greeting Card*.
[7] *Grief* Page 56 Written September 11, 2001 as the radio poured out the grim news of the Terrorist Attack. Published in *Saugeen City News* September 2001 and *The Interim* October 2001.

[8] ***Shared Tears*** Page 58 Written when a suicide left a seven year old without her Daddy. Published and sold as a *Greeting Card*.
[9] ***The Echo of My Weeping*** Page 61 Written on hearing the news of a three year old child killed in a farm accident – one month after the death of our Grandson. Published and sold as a *Greeting Card*.
[10] ***Love Revealed*** Page 70 Published in *The Durham Chronicle* December 1994 and in *The Interim* December 1997. Published and sold as a *Greeting Card*.
[11] ***No Vacancy*** Page 72 Published in *The Hanover Post* December 2002. Published and sold as a *Greeting Card*
[12] ***Nitroglycerin*** Page 86 Published in *The Fellowship Link* January 2004. Published and sold as a *Greeting Card*.

About the Author

Brian Austin and his wife live on a small acreage at Durham, Ontario, Canada. They have three grown children and two grandchildren. They also eagerly await a reunion with a grandson whom they have never yet had the opportunity to hold.

Author's Note

Although not intentionally a collection of "religious" poetry, many of these poems refer to my faith in God. That faith is an integral part of who I am, thus it is without apology that I allow it to speak through my work.

I have not set out to "convert" any readers, yet it is my express hope than any and all references to God in this collection would make Him attractive – someone you would wish to meet if you could believe He was real. I apologize for the "religious language" that at times slips into my writing. I do not apologize for the firm convictions behind that language.

The works in this volume that mean the most to me are those ones that come out of my own struggles as a very imperfect Christian in an imperfect world. A number of them express deep pain and aching questions.

I do not pretend to have all the answers. I trust that within the very questioning and heart-cry of some of these works, you will find something that will resonate in your heart and mind.

To order additional copies of this book or the companion audio CD, take these ISBN numbers to your favorite bookstore. If they don't have them in stock they can quickly order them. You can also purchase on-line.

    Laughter & Tears (Trade Paper) ISBN 1-894928-66-0
    Laughter & Tears (Audio CD)   ISBN 1-894928-67-9

Printed in the United States
38227LVS00001B/1-204